St John's Advent books refreshingly
range of people associated with the
inspiringly wide range of styles and
fresh insights into scripture, and how
live it out each day. *All Things New* continues this excellent tradition.
The Rt Revd Paul Butler, Bishop of Southwell and Nottingham

If you are looking for a series that is both seasonal and challenging
then *All Things New* is surely a handy, useful and reflective series of
meditations. I was struck by its style and approach. It is arranged
thematically, building on each week's theme in a way that takes the
reader on a personal journey of faith. The daily readings draw upon
the real-life faith journeys of a variety of contributors from students
to staff, and various ministry experiences in different contexts. This
brings much meaning to the theme of each week. The essence
of each passage for reflection is drawn out in a most relevant
way, and the questions and guides for self-reflection truly aid a
contemplative and reflective spirituality.
Roshan Mendis, Asia Chairperson, Micah Network

These readings and devotionals will provide you with a valuable
tool to pause and reflect on God's truth throughout the busy
Advent season. This is a great and welcome resource for all who
long for a greater depth in their relationship with Jesus.
Mike Pilavachi, Director of Soul Survivor

Each year I look forward to the Advent book produced by students
and staff of St John's, Nottingham. It never fails to live up to
expectations, enabling our Advent discipline by offering daily Bible
readings, reflections and prayers. We find ourselves challenged and
encouraged by reflections that come from thoughtful, creative and
sometimes quirky perspectives, which help us to look and think
afresh. The theme of *All Things New* could not be more apposite for
the church and our communities at this time. In the Advent season
of waiting and longing, this book will be a daily friend and guide.
Ven Canon Jackie Searle, Archdeacon of Gloucester

This set of reflections and readings for Advent will be an excellent
guide to this important time of the Church's year. It offers a variety
of perspectives which will enrich the reader a great deal.
Revd Dr Graham Tomlin, Dean, St Mellitus College

*And the one who was seated on the throne said, 'See I am making **all things new'**.*

Revelation 21.5

Kindle version of this book

For the first time St John's are pleased to offer this Advent book in Kindle format from the Amazon.co.uk store.

For more information please see http://stjohns-nottm.ac.uk/ab2012

AllThings
New

Scripture quotations are from the New Revised
Standard Version of the Bible, copyright 1989, 1995
by the Division of Christian Education
of the National Council of
Churches of Christ in the USA.

Used by permission. All rights reserved.

Cover designed by Sian Puckrin

British Library Cataloguing in Publication data

A catalogue record for this book
is available from the British Library

ISBN 978-1-900920-20-9

Typeset by Martin Barrett
St John's College Nottingham

Printed and bound by
Stirland Paterson Print Group
Ilkeston

AllThings
New

**Daily readings for
Advent and Christmas**

St John's
NOTTINGHAM
Creative Christian Learning

Thank you...

A big thank you is due to all the St John's College Nottingham members who have contributed to this volume. Their names will become apparent as you travel through its pages. Many contributions were produced during an extremely busy term, so, thank you.

This book is also available for the first time electronically. A big 'thank you' goes to Gareth Regan for his contribution to the Kindle project.

The book could not have come together without the wise guidance of Helen Taylor and the computing expertise of Martin Barrett. Both of you put in commitment beyond the call of duty. Thank you for your assistance and support.

Kate Byrom and **Ian Paul**
Editors

Kate is a second year ordinand and Ian is Dean of Studies.

Contents

How to use this book

What follows in these pages are five weeks of daily readings to take you through Advent and Christmas. The readings are not exhaustive studies of the passage in question, but simply provide a perspective to stimulate further thought and prayer.

It is recommended that you take time prayerfully to work through the Bible reading for each day and the reflection that follows. **Ponder** points and a **Prayer** are often included to stimulate further thought and response. After each set of six reflections there is a 'free' day per week entitled **Review and reflect.** This breathing space is to provide catch-up time if needed, and a chance to allow God to speak further. You might use these pages to capture insights you are keen to remember.

Introduction

When I started in post as Principal of St John's College earlier this year, several tasks awaited me. Few, however, were as easy as confirming the production of this, our annual Advent Book. For several years now St John's has helped to deepen the spiritual and theological understanding of thousands as they have used this resource to guide them through the rich themes of the Advent season, and it is clear from the feedback we have received that the ministry offered through this volume is greatly appreciated.

Advent is most widely associated, of course, with preparing for Christmas. The birth of Jesus is a momentous event, and merits attention on more than just one, festive day per year. That is why since the sixth century the Church has commended the month or so leading up to Christmas Day as a period of reflection on the broader significance of the adventus or 'coming' of Christ. Over time this has led to the allocation of certain Sundays in the season to linked topics such as the foreshadowing of the nativity in Old Testament patriarchs and prophets, the ministry of John the Baptist, and the witness of Jesus's mother, Mary. More generally, though, Advent has provided an opportunity to focus not only on the birth but also on the return or 'second coming' of Christ featured so prominently in the Gospels, Acts and Epistles (Mk 13; Matt 24—5; Acts 1.11; 3.21; 1 Thess 4.15—17; Phil 3.20). This promised event matters not only because it will confirm Jesus's rule and reign over the world as we know it; vitally, it will also usher in a new age—an age in which evil, sin and death are forever expunged in a new heaven and a new earth.

Advent, then, is ultimately about renewal. That is why we felt it appropriate to mark a new phase in the life of St John's with a book focused on this profoundly important subject. Liturgically, Advent has long heralded the start of a new church year. It has also been presented as a penitential season—a period of repentance and reflection in which we are called to renew our commitment to Christ the coming King. Yet it is Scripture which offers the fullest and most definitive guide to renewal, and to its embodiment in the Saviour who was born among us, and who will return in glory.

Hence in this book, faculty, staff and friends of St John's explore a wide range of Old and New Testament texts related variously to the renewing God, the renewal of God's people, the renewal of the earth, personal renewal and the renewal of hope. Our own hope is that the reflections which follow in these pages will inspire you to renewed faith in Christ, renewed prayer, and renewed zeal for ministry and mission.

Grace and peace,

David Hilborn
Principal, St John's College, Nottingham

God: the source of new life

Week One

Peering into the void... again

Sunday 2 December

Genesis 1.1-5, 26-31

[1] In the beginning when God created the heavens and the earth, [2] the earth was a formless void and darkness covered the face of the deep, while a wind from God swept over the face of the waters. [3] Then God said, 'Let there be light'; and there was light. [4] And God saw that the light was good; and God separated the light from the darkness. [5] God called the light Day, and the darkness he called Night. And there was evening and there was morning, the first day […]

[26] Then God said, 'Let us make humankind in our image, according to our likeness; and let them have dominion over the fish of the sea, and over the birds of the air, and over the cattle, and over all the wild animals of the earth, and over every creeping thing that creeps upon the earth.'

> [27] So God created humankind in his image,
> in the image of God he created them;
> male and female he created them.

[28] God blessed them, and God said to them, 'Be fruitful and multiply, and fill the earth and subdue it; and have dominion over the fish of the sea and over the birds of the air and over every living thing that moves upon the earth.' [29] God said, 'See, I have given you every plant yielding seed that is upon the face of all the earth, and every tree with seed in its fruit; you shall have them for food. [30] And to every beast of the earth, and to every bird of the air, and to everything that creeps on the earth, everything that has the breath of life, I have given every green plant for food.' And it was so. [31] God saw everything that he had made, and indeed, it was very good.

Prayer

Holy God and Father of all humankind,
Loom over me,
Peer into me,
Bring your light again.
Where there is darkness
Speak again your word into our world.
All this and more we ask in Jesus's name.

Then God said, 'let there be light'.

The De Laurentis movie *In the Beginning* starts with a dark screen, a narrator's voice and a pin-point of light which begins to grow. This sequence stays with me when I think about God acting in the world and in our lives, creating, forming and renewing. I have also held on to this picture when I think about the chaos in our world and the chaos in our lives.

The earth was a formless void and darkness covered the face of the deep.

Have you ever looked into a situation and found a place of such discomfort and wondered when it ends?

And so it starts. There is a story, a journey, an order and a process. God leans, hovers, broods and speaks and then…there is light. God speaks and the world becomes. Out of nothing…something. And the something is very good. It takes time and leads to a moment where humanity is there beside God.

Our hope for renewal is founded on this creator God who is the origin of life itself.

When we find ourselves in chaos, in a place of darkness or wildness, in this place of uncertainty, I think it is natural to ask what God is doing. When I am in this place I have to remember that God renews, reforms, persists. I imagine an expectant God, who looms overwhelmingly over the formless, chaotic aspects of my life. He is focused, breathing on this emptiness inside of me. If this is where you are, I don't want to be blasé about your chaos. I simply want to say, he is looking intently and there can be light again.

Ponder

Where do you hope for renewal in your life or the world around? Bring your longings before the source of life.

Bola Adamolekun

Bola is a second year ordinand at St John's, with an interest in creativity and spirituality.

Wings like eagles

Monday 3 December

Isaiah 40.25–31

[25] To whom then will you compare me,
   or who is my equal? says the Holy One.
[26] Lift up your eyes on high and see:
   Who created these?
He who brings out their host and numbers them,
   calling them all by name;
because he is great in strength,
   mighty in power,
   not one is missing.
[27] Why do you say, O Jacob,
   and speak, O Israel,
'My way is hidden from the LORD,
   and my right is disregarded by my God'?
[28] Have you not known? Have you not heard?
The LORD is the everlasting God,
   the Creator of the ends of the earth.
He does not faint or grow weary;
   his understanding is unsearchable.
[29] He gives power to the faint,
   and strengthens the powerless.
[30] Even youths will faint and be weary,
   and the young will fall exhausted;
[31] but those who wait for the LORD
   shall renew their strength,
   they shall mount up with wings like eagles,
they shall run and not be weary,
   they shall walk and not faint.

Prayer

Lord, into our busyness speak your peace and stillness.

I have a self-help book that promises to improve my parenting skills in just one hour. Knowing what I do about family life (and my own faults and foibles), I suspect it might take longer! Short cuts to success play to our desires to have it all and have it now. As attractive as they might seem, we sense that their promises are cheap. Not every problem or desire can be addressed by a quick fix.

In this reading, the writer exhorts God's people to wait for the Lord.

Waiting is hard to do. As I waited recently for a delayed meeting, my emotions went from self-important resentment about wasted time, to boredom, to frustration over the things I would rather be doing. While we wait we have no control. While we wait our power to direct and manipulate are relinquished. While we wait all the initiative rests with God.

I sense the writer's exasperation that some doubt that God sees, or cares, or is interested in their concerns: 'Have you not known? Have you not heard?', he implores, 'The Lord is the everlasting God'. This God is worth waiting for. His is the only power that can save. His promises to renew the strength of the weary are not empty, but true.

The most precious things cannot be rushed. The gestation of a baby. The maturing of love. A touch from God. The promise is sure; 'those who wait for the Lord shall renew their strength, they shall mount up with wings like eagles, they shall run and not be weary, they shall walk and not faint.'

Ponder

How good are you at putting down tasks and busyness to simply be with God, waiting for his initiative?

How will you protect time to 'wait for the Lord' during the busy season of Advent?

Kate Byrom

Kate is a second year ordinand grappling with the balance of busyness and stillness, activity and contemplation.

God with us: A present presence

Tuesday 4 December

Matthew 1.18–25

[18] Now the birth of Jesus the Messiah took place in this way. When his mother Mary had been engaged to Joseph, but before they lived together, she was found to be with child from the Holy Spirit. [19] Her husband Joseph, being a righteous man and unwilling to expose her to public disgrace, planned to dismiss her quietly. [20] But just when he had resolved to do this, an angel of the Lord appeared to him in a dream and said, 'Joseph, son of David, do not be afraid to take Mary as your wife, for the child conceived in her is from the Holy Spirit. [21] She will bear a son, and you are to name him Jesus, for he will save his people from their sins.' [22] All this took place to fulfil what had been spoken by the Lord through the prophet:

[23] 'Look, the virgin shall conceive and bear a son,
   and they shall name him Emmanuel',

which means, 'God is with us.' [24] When Joseph awoke from sleep, he did as the angel of the Lord commanded him; he took her as his wife, [25] but had no marital relations with her until she had borne a son; and he named him Jesus.

Prayer

Emmanuel, as you continue to break into history's pages, would you illuminate the words of your story. Thank you that we can continue to know your presence with us today through your Holy Spirit.

They had been waiting a long time; a very long time. Many were clinging to the prophecies they dared to hope would one day be fulfilled. They had heard through the prophets about a Messiah—a child will come, they had said, to save his people. Others were thinking sceptically 'I believed it once', but their hope was waning.

Then it happened. Few were watching and few were aware. But the words of the prophet were being fulfilled. God with us; Emmanuel.

He was here; with no pomp and with all the vulnerability of a baby. Born to a teenage mother who was betrothed to a man not his father. The King of Kings had the most inauspicious start to life on earth. But God had come to walk amongst his people once again; the people into whom he had once breathed life, in a garden long ago. The Creator became a creature. The infinite became finite. The eternal God became confined to a particular time, place and people.

His life, and death, would change everything.

Through his Holy Spirit, God is still here with us—intimately involved with his people, identifying with our challenges and sharing our suffering. His presence ushers new life into the here and now. The source of our hope is still Emmanuel; God with us.

Ponder

Simply look again and be amazed at each detail of these events.

The promise of God's presence is as true today as it was on the first day that Jesus's eyes opened on our earth. In what ways are you aware of God's Spirit with and in you?

Meditate on the words 'God is with us'. Bring to mind each area of your life, work and relationships as you do this, honouring God as the source of hope and renewal.

Matthew Thomas

Matthew is a musician and intercessor, living on site in the St John's community with his wife Gabrielle, an ordinand.

Walking with life

Wednesday 5 December

John 1.1–13

[1] In the beginning was the Word, and the Word was with God, and the Word was God. [2] He was in the beginning with God. [3] All things came into being through him, and without him not one thing came into being. What has come into being [4] in him was life, and the life was the light of all people. [5] The light shines in the darkness, and the darkness did not overcome it.

[6] There was a man sent from God, whose name was John. [7] He came as a witness to testify to the light, so that all might believe through him. [8] He himself was not the light, but he came to testify to the light. [9] The true light, which enlightens everyone, was coming into the world.

[10] He was in the world, and the world came into being through him; yet the world did not know him. [11] He came to what was his own, and his own people did not accept him. [12] But to all who received him, who believed in his name, he gave power to become children of God, [13] who were born, not of blood or of the will of the flesh or of the will of man, but of God.

[14] And the Word became flesh and lived among us, and we have seen his glory, the glory as of a father's only son, full of grace and truth. [15] (John testified to him and cried out, 'This was he of whom I said, "He who comes after me ranks ahead of me because he was before me."') [16] From his fullness we have all received, grace upon grace. [17] The law indeed was given through Moses; grace and truth came through Jesus Christ. [18] No one has ever seen God. It is God the only Son, who is close to the Father's heart, who has made him known.

Prayer

Light of the world, as I walk through this day may I find strength in your presence and light to overcome the darkness. With each step I take, release your life in mine and release your life in the world.

Imagine John as he recorded these words, words about the one who is the Word of God. Imagine him reflecting on the time he had spent with Jesus, walking with him and listening to him. Imagine John realizing that with Jesus he was in the presence of the creator and sustainer of all life.

All the life John witnessed was given and sustained by Jesus—the fish that filled his nets, the stars in the sky, the quiet and the storms of Galilee, the plants beside the way, the people who came to Jesus and went away renewed. In Jesus is the source of all life.

But then…

The Word became flesh and lived among us.

In Jesus God was suddenly here. The creator of the universe was close enough to see, touch, smell, hear. Here was God, breathing, eating, speaking, weeping, teaching.

Having walked with this Jesus, John invited his readers to come and meet him themselves. His desire was not that we should be observers, but that we would also walk with Christ—that we should 'walk in the light' (1 John 1.7).

Ponder

What will walking with Christ today involve for you?

Peter Franklin

Peter is an architect by profession, an Extension Studies Student with St John's and a Reader in the Church of England, exploring the way forward in his life and ministry.

Blinded by the light

Thursday 6 December

Acts 9.1–9

[9] Meanwhile Saul, still breathing threats and murder against the disciples of the Lord, went to the high priest [2] and asked him for letters to the synagogues at Damascus, so that if he found any who belonged to the Way, men or women, he might bring them bound to Jerusalem. [3] Now as he was going along and approaching Damascus, suddenly a light from heaven flashed around him. [4] He fell to the ground and heard a voice saying to him, 'Saul, Saul, why do you persecute me?' [5] He asked, 'Who are you, Lord?' The reply came, 'I am Jesus, whom you are persecuting. [6] But get up and enter the city, and you will be told what you are to do.' [7] The men who were travelling with him stood speechless because they heard the voice but saw no one. [8] Saul got up from the ground, and though his eyes were open, he could see nothing; so they led him by the hand and brought him into Damascus. [9] For three days he was without sight, and neither ate nor drank.

Prayer

Lighten our darkness, we beseech thee, O Lord…

On Winter afternoons my young son delights in taking up strange stances in front of the church floodlights so that monstrous shadows are cast on the old stone tower they illuminate. These menacing figures, dark projections of his body shape, are a product of the light. How often, as we encounter the light of the risen Christ, are we more aware of our personal shadows, our sinfulness?

Saul, the persecutor, saw the risen Christ, in all his resplendent glory, on the road to Damascus and was plunged into a deep darkness—a place to reflect on the spiritual bankruptcy of his condition and the call of the light. Luke describes that other great church leader, Simon, encountering the power of Jesus in the miraculous catch of fish. His response was to fall at Jesus's knees and say; "Go away from me, Lord: I am a sinful man!" (Luke 5.8) In each case the Lord renamed these men, Paul and Peter, and gave them tasks which would require obedience and trust.

I once saw the face of Christ... it came to me when a speaker was calling for intercessors and I was crippled by a sense of personal sin and inadequacy. I will never forget the eyes of love which both drew me in and washed me clean, so that I could rise and respond.

We should not be surprised if encounter with God, source of light and love, makes us more painfully aware of our own darkness and lack of love…. It is often exactly when we are 'breathing out angry threats' that Christ, the Prince of Peace, meets us! No matter; this account teaches us that the light of the risen Christ has the power to penetrate our personal darkness and his love can transform us to walk, in obedience and trust, the path to which he calls us.

Becky Richards

Becky is a part-time ordinand at St John's and mother of three.

I am not ashamed

Friday 7 December

2 Timothy 1.8–14

[8] Do not be ashamed, then, of the testimony about our Lord or of me his prisoner, but join with me in suffering for the gospel, relying on the power of God, [9] who saved us and called us with a holy calling, not according to our works but according to his own purpose and grace. This grace was given to us in Christ Jesus before the ages began, [10] but it has now been revealed through the appearing of our Saviour Christ Jesus, who abolished death and brought life and immortality to light through the gospel. [11] For this gospel I was appointed a herald and an apostle and a teacher, [12] and for this reason I suffer as I do. But I am not ashamed, for I know the one in whom I have put my trust, and I am sure that he is able to guard until that day what I have entrusted to him. [13] Hold to the standard of sound teaching that you have heard from me, in the faith and love that are in Christ Jesus. [14] Guard the good treasure entrusted to you, with the help of the Holy Spirit living in us.

Prayer

Heavenly Father, you have brought us from death to life through your Son our Saviour Jesus Christ. Give us grace to live our lives in the hope and truth of the gospel that we may not be silenced by shame but testify to the transforming power of Jesus.

Shame silences; the shame of our ignorance of the faith, the shame of others' ridicule, the shame we feel when the faith is brought into disrepute. Prison is a shameful experience in any culture, not least in Paul's. Yet from his prison cell he roundly declares, "I am not ashamed." This is not because he is thick-skinned or without conscience, but because of the gospel—in which the world's estimation of power and weakness, shame and honour have been reversed. Jesus Christ through the shame of a criminal's death has ended the reign of death and by the power of the resurrection has opened the door to a destiny none would have dreamed of—immortality: the resurrection of the body.

So Paul offers the antidote to the silence of shame—the grace of the gospel and testimony to Jesus in the face of suffering. And he encourages timid Timothy to practice two disciplines that will help him to find voice in the face of the shaming words and actions of others: trust and faithfulness.

Trust (v.12): living in the present with the assurance of the future; the great day is coming.

Faithfulness (v.13—14): holding to the truth of the gospel and letting it speak into our lives and to the world in which we live, by the power of the Holy Spirit; the treasure is for sharing.

These are not practices that we can turn on at a moment's notice when trouble comes; they are habits of life developed by prayer, study, reflection and action, which gradually become more and more a part of us as we pray for them and live them. Paul shares his own testimony to the truth of this with Timothy; but Timothy must seek it for himself.

Ponder

How might your prayer life (on your own and with others) help you to live daily in the light of God's future?

How might you develop habits of study (on your own and with others) that will help you to understand how the truth of the gospel speaks to life in today's world?

Revd Nick Ladd

Nick is Dean of College at St John's and has had over twenty years in parish ministry.

Review and reflect

What have you learned this week about God, the source of renewal?

How will you create space this Advent to encounter God afresh?

Are there things you need to take up? Are there things you need to lay down to meet God anew?

Renewing God's
Week Two people

God will do anything for his people

Sunday 9 December

Exodus 33.17–34.7

[17] The LORD said to Moses, 'I will do the very thing that you have asked; for you have found favour in my sight, and I know you by name.' [18] Moses said, 'Show me your glory, I pray.' [19] And he said, 'I will make all my goodness pass before you, and will proclaim before you the name, "The LORD"; and I will be gracious to whom I will be gracious, and will show mercy on whom I will show mercy. [20] But', he said, 'you cannot see my face; for no one shall see me and live.' [21] And the LORD continued, 'See, there is a place by me where you shall stand on the rock; [22] and while my glory passes by I will put you in a cleft of the rock, and I will cover you with my hand until I have passed by; [23] then I will take away my hand, and you shall see my back; but my face shall not be seen.'

[34:1] The LORD said to Moses, 'Cut two tablets of stone like the former ones, and I will write on the tablets the words that were on the former tablets, which you broke. [2] Be ready in the morning, and come up in the morning to Mount Sinai and present yourself there to me, on the top of the mountain. [3] No one shall come up with you, and do not let anyone be seen throughout all the mountain; and do not let flocks or herds graze in front of that mountain.' [4] So Moses cut two tablets of stone like the former ones; and he rose early in the morning and went up on Mount Sinai, as the LORD had commanded him, and took in his hand the two tablets of stone. [5] The LORD descended in the cloud and stood with him there, and proclaimed the name, 'The LORD.' [6] The LORD passed before him, and proclaimed,

'The LORD, the LORD,
a God merciful and gracious,
slow to anger,
and abounding in steadfast love and faithfulness,
[7] keeping steadfast love for the thousandth generation,
forgiving iniquity and transgression and sin,
yet by no means clearing the guilty,
but visiting the iniquity of the parents
upon the children and the children's children,
to the third and the fourth generation.'

Prayer

Heavenly Father, thank you for loving your people so much that you would do anything for us. Lord, renew your church, and help us to be the people you have created us to be.

There can scarcely be a more satisfying response to a request than, 'for you I'll do anything'. So imagine how Moses felt when God himself gave him this reply (v. 17).

Moses had been interceding on behalf of God's people in the wake of their idolatrous creation and worship of a golden calf. Initially, God had told Moses that he would no longer be with them on their journey to Canaan but through Moses' mediation the Lord relented. What a great advert for the power of prayer!

When Moses then asked to see God's glory it was no self-indulgent request for a supernatural experience, but a heartfelt plea for the Lord to renew the Covenant that his people had broken through their idolatry. Moses recognised that only a manifestation of the very nature of God would be sufficient to restore it. Thus, the renewal of the Covenant is above all a revelation of 'a God merciful and gracious, slow to anger, and abounding in steadfast love and faithfulness…forgiving iniquity and transgression and sin'.

Of course, it is out of this same nature that God sent his Son to die for the sins of the world. And in our amazement of what he has done for us, if we listen carefully we hear him speaking to us: 'for you I'll do anything'.

Ponder

We place much value on *personal* belief and repentance in the way we think about salvation. Yet in the two most dramatic appearances of God in the world—here in this passage and in the life of Jesus—we see God intervening on behalf of *all* His people.

How might an understanding that God renews *corporately* shape our understanding of what church is? How does it affect our mission?

Ian Jamieson

Ian is a second year student at St John's and an ordinand from the Diocese of Wakefield.

The desert blooms

Monday10 December

Isaiah 35.1–7, 10

[1] The wilderness and the dry land shall be glad,
    the desert shall rejoice and blossom;
  like the crocus [2] it shall blossom abundantly,
    and rejoice with joy and singing.
  The glory of Lebanon shall be given to it,
    the majesty of Carmel and Sharon.
  They shall see the glory of the LORD,
    the majesty of our God.

[3] Strengthen the weak hands,
    and make firm the feeble knees.
[4] Say to those who are of a fearful heart,
  'Be strong, do not fear!
  Here is your God.
    He will come with vengeance,
    with terrible recompense.
  He will come and save you.'

[5] Then the eyes of the blind shall be opened,
    and the ears of the deaf unstopped;
[6] then the lame shall leap like a deer,
    and the tongue of the speechless sing for joy.
  for waters shall break forth in the wilderness,
    and streams in the desert;
[7] the burning sand shall become a pool,
  and the thirsty ground springs of water;
    the haunt of jackals shall become a swamp,
  the grass shall become reeds and rushes […]

[10] And the ransomed of the LORD shall return,
    and come to Zion with singing;
  everlasting joy shall be upon their heads;
    they shall obtain joy and gladness,
  and sorrow and sighing shall flee away.

Prayer

God who made the desert bloom, renew your people that they might sing your praises and make your glory known.

I love watching television series about the natural world, and one of the scenes I remember most came from a programme about deserts. The land looked dry and parched, and then, from some distant place where rains had fallen, came first a trickle of water, which grew into a flood. As if by magic, bright flowers bloomed where there had been nothing but parched earth as dry as dust. We had a smaller scale magical experience a few years ago in the field opposite college. The farmer had stopped using chemicals, and suddenly the whole field bloomed with poppies. It was so dramatic it made the news!

Isaiah sees a similarly dramatic transformation in the fortunes of God's people. They are in exile, struggling to make pilgrimage to their home city of Jerusalem, threatened by their former neighbours in Edom. Their spiritual and national life is as dry as dust. Yet God's dramatic intervention changes everything. The desert through which they trudge becomes a fertile valley. The places of fear now speak of peace. What was drudgery is now a source of joy. All this is the work of the one who makes the blind to see, the deaf to hear, the lame to walk—this is good news to tell far and wide (Matt 11.4–5)!

Yet this good news brings judgement—not only for Edom, but also for God's people themselves. This is a highway of holiness, where there is no place for the unclean or profane. In every age, the renewal of God's people is a renewal of holiness as well as a renewal of life, as we welcome among us the Holy One of Israel. Blessed indeed is the one who does not stumble on account of him (Matt 11.6).

Ponder

Where do you see God's people struggling today, in your country, in your town or village?

What might it mean to see the renewing water of God's presence for them? Where would this bring joy? Where might it bring judgement?

Revd Dr Ian Paul

Ian trained at St John's and was in church leadership for 10 years before returning to the college in 2004. He is Dean of Studies and teaches New Testament and preaching.

Lament until our days are renewed

Tuesday 11 December

Lamentations 5

[5] Remember, O LORD, what has befallen us;
 look, and see our disgrace!
[8] Slaves rule over us;
 there is no one to deliver us from their hand.
[9] We get our bread at the peril of our lives,
 because of the sword in the wilderness.
[10] Our skin is black as an oven
 from the scorching heat of famine.
[11] Women are raped in Zion,
 virgins in the towns of Judah.
[12] Princes are hung up by their hands;
 no respect is shown to the elders.
[13] Young men are compelled to grind,
 and boys stagger under loads of wood.
[14] The old men have left the city gate,
 the young men their music.
[15] The joy of our hearts has ceased;
 our dancing has been turned to mourning.
[16] The crown has fallen from our head;
 woe to us, for we have sinned!
[17] Because of this our hearts are sick,
 because of these things our eyes have grown dim:
[18] because of Mount Zion, which lies desolate;
 jackals prowl over it.

[19] But you, O LORD, reign for ever;
 your throne endures to all generations.
[20] Why have you forgotten us completely?
 Why have you forsaken us these many days?
[21] Restore us to yourself, O LORD, that we may be restored;
 renew our days as of old—
[22] unless you have utterly rejected us,
 and are angry with us beyond measure.

Prayer

Lord God, help us be fully aware of your saving presence during the toughest times in our lives. Help us realise that you are the source of light in the darkness. Allow us to embrace your Holy Spirit and find renewal.

People can moan a lot. We see this generally in life today and in the Bible.

Here the Israelites lament to God about the loss of Jerusalem and how their captors mistreat them. They have a lot to moan about! They state the sins that have been performed against them and plead with the Lord to remember those dark deeds. They ask some simple questions that all those of faith might ask. Why do you forget us? Why do you forsake us for so long?

When life gets tough we can run to God with what has happened, just as the Israelites lamented their lot. It is no surprise that the Israelites brought their dire concerns to God; they knew what God was like. They had once been slaves in Egypt and God had delivered them. He took them into the land of milk and honey, and fulfilled his promise. However, the Israelites seemed never to stay on top. They were invaded and once again forced into slavery.

Life can be hard, whether in church, work, family, ministry or personally. During these times we often cry out to the Lord and tell him our woes. We ask God why it is happening. The writer of this passage sees that God is with his people. When we are down in the dumps we should remember this; whenever God's chosen people have faced hardship and been oppressed he rescues and renews. He is the one to whom we can cry out 'restore us to yourself, O Lord, that we might be restored'.

Ponder

If you were writing a lament for God's people today, what would be the nature of its woes and complaints?

Hold up the people of God in prayer to the only one who can restore and renew us.

Chris Dommett

Chris is studying Youth and Community Work with Practical Theology at St John's and works with Ashby Youth For Christ.

What's in a name?

Wednesday 12 December

Matthew 16.13-20

[13] Now when Jesus came into the district of Caesarea Philippi, he asked his disciples, 'Who do people say that the Son of Man is?' [14] And they said, 'Some say John the Baptist, but others Elijah, and still others Jeremiah or one of the prophets.' [15] He said to them, 'But who do you say that I am?' [16] Simon Peter answered, 'You are the Messiah, the Son of the living God.' [17] And Jesus answered him, 'Blessed are you, Simon son of Jonah! For flesh and blood has not revealed this to you, but my Father in heaven. [18] And I tell you, you are Peter, and on this rock I will build my church, and the gates of Hades will not prevail against it. [19] I will give you the keys of the kingdom of heaven, and whatever you bind on earth will be bound in heaven, and whatever you loose on earth will be loosed in heaven.' [20] Then he sternly ordered the disciples not to tell anyone that he was the Messiah.

Prayer

Lord Jesus, you know me by name, you have saved me and restored me in relationship with our heavenly father. Help me to be renewed daily, hear your call to serve your church and have the courage to do your will, in Christ's name.

Many couples at college have been blessed with new babies this year and might well have searched through baby naming books to find the right name. When our son was born, Joshua was quite an unusual name, but now 18 years on we find others thought the same and it seems quite common. Of course Joshua has the same root as the name Jesus, meaning 'The Lord is salvation'.

In this passage we explore the name of Jesus a bit more. His self-designation as Son of Man seems deliberately ambiguous. It partly refers to his humanity and present activities, but could be linked to his heavenly nature (see Daniel 7.13–14) or his suffering and dying. Some identified him as a prophet, which he certainly was, bringing a message of judgement on injustice and liberty for the oppressed, but he was so much more than that.

Peter gets it right: Jesus is the Messiah, the Christ, the bringer of salvation. He is more than an ordinary man; he is the Son of the living God. Jesus is fully human, suffering and dying for us; and fully divine, with the power to overcome sin and death. Indeed, 'God gave him the name that is above every name, so that at the name of Jesus, every knee should bow' (Philippians 2.9–10).

Peter has declared Jesus's true significance; now Jesus in turn discloses where Peter stands in the working out of God's purpose. He reveals the significance of Peter's name: the Rock on which Jesus will build his church. It describes not his character (for we know from his threefold denial of Jesus how shaky that was) but rather his function, the foundation stone of the community of the followers of Christ.

Ponder

Where do you stand? Who do you say Jesus is?

What function in his church, the community of believers, has Jesus called you to?

Chris Youngman

Chris completed his ordination training at St John's in June 2012 and is now serving as a curate in Radcliffe-on-Trent, near Nottingham.

A call to accountability

Thursday 13 December

Matthew 18.15-20

[15] 'If another member of the church sins against you, go and point out the fault when the two of you are alone. If the member listens to you, you have regained that one. [16]But if you are not listened to, take one or two others along with you, so that every word may be confirmed by the evidence of two or three witnesses. [17]If the member refuses to listen to them, tell it to the church; and if the offender refuses to listen even to the church, let such a one be to you as a Gentile and a tax-collector. [18]Truly I tell you, whatever you bind on earth will be bound in heaven, and whatever you loose on earth will be loosed in heaven. [19]Again, truly I tell you, if two of you agree on earth about anything you ask, it will be done for you by my Father in heaven. [20]For where two or three are gathered in my name, I am there among them.'

Prayer

Lord, make me an instrument of your love and peace. Give me the wisdom and courage to reach out to those in need of healing and reconciliation.

At some point in our lives most of us find ourselves in conflict with another, sometimes over small, petty things and sometimes larger, more difficult conflicts, including anger and aggression. How good it is that we can turn to the Bible for help. Jesus was very clear on how we should go about this tricky business of seeking reconciliation.

The first step is to seek out privately the person who has offended us and explain the fault. In Jesus's time, this was required under the law (Leviticus 19.17). If we want to settle a difference, we need to do it face-to-face, and in most cases, a little friendly conversation will set the matter right.

If this friendly conversation fails, Jesus tells us to bring in another person, not to put the offender on trial, but to try and persuade him or her to see the wrong that has been committed and be reconciled.

If the matter is then still not resolved, Jesus tells us to seek the help of the Christian community. Our fellow Christians should pray and seek a solution for reconciliation which is based on Christian love and wisdom.

If this fails, what then? Jesus seems to say that we have the right to abandon stubborn offenders and treat them as social outcasts. The tax collectors and Gentiles were regarded as 'unclean' by the religious-minded Jews. However, things are not that cut and dried. We know from the Gospel accounts that Jesus often had fellowship with tax collectors; he ate with them and even praised them on occasion. Jesus refuses no one who is ready to receive pardon, healing and restoration. The call to accountability is inevitable and we cannot escape it, neither in this life nor at the Day of Judgment.

While we have the opportunity, we must make every effort to win stubborn offenders with the grace and power of God. This is not an easy thing to do, but it is what God calls us to. We must never give up on anyone.

Ponder

Do you tolerate broken relationships or do you seek to repair them as God gives you the opportunity to mend and restore what is broken?

With whom could you take fresh steps toward reconciliation today?

Sue Vornhagen

Sue is British but has been resident in Germany for over 30 years. She is studying on the distance learning course at St John's.

I am chosen, I am free

Friday 14 December

1 Peter 2.9-12

[9] But you are a chosen race, a royal priesthood, a holy nation, God's own people, in order that you may proclaim the mighty acts of him who called you out of darkness into his marvellous light.

[10] Once you were not a people,
    but now you are God's people;
  once you had not received mercy,
    but now you have received mercy.
[11] Beloved, I urge you as aliens and exiles to abstain from the desires of the flesh that wage war against the soul. [12] Conduct yourselves honourably among the Gentiles, so that, though they malign you as evildoers, they may see your honourable deeds and glorify God when he comes to judge.

Prayer

Thank you for choosing me. Help me, and all your people, to faithfully represent you wherever we are today.

How does it feel to be chosen? To be chosen to represent one's country in a sporting event or at a national occasion must be an immense privilege. How must it feel to be the one selected out of all the other potential team members or representatives?

What Peter is writing about here is so much more even than this. He was writing to a scattered audience living across a wide range of areas in what is now called Turkey. To be set apart as God's chosen people amidst a pagan culture must have been mind-blowing. What a comfort and inspiration!

This letter was written as an encouragement, but also to provide guidance. Living amidst a culture that largely ignored their new-found faith, Peter tried to ensure that those who would accuse the followers of Jesus of any misdemeanours would have no grounds on which to base their accusations. Christians were, and still are, an easy target for criticism, especially where there is evidence of failing to practise what we preach. Living out the gospel publicly, authentically and with integrity is essential. Saying one thing and doing another is not an option if we want to live as God intends.

God has made a choice…he has chosen us! But this leaves us with choices of our own. In the final Harry Potter book Dumbledore tells Harry, 'It is our choices that show what we truly are, far more than our abilities'. God is not interested in what we can or cannot do; he is interested in who we are. Choosing to live counter-culturally, within a world that champions selfish individualism over selfless community, and shallow gratification over self-control, signals to others that our priorities are different. Our priorities are God's priorities and not the world's.

Ponder

How does it feel to know that, with your fellow believers, we are chosen and set apart by God?

How easy is it for people who do not know Christ to see in you what it means to be a Christian?

What would need to change for you to better represent Jesus in your daily life? How can Christians together help each other with this?

Louise Tinniswood

Louise was a student at St John's between 2010 and 2012, and is now Curate at Holy Trinity and St. Oswald's, Finningley and St. Saviour's, Auckley, Doncaster.

Review and reflect

_____

_____

_____

_____

_____

_____

_____

_____

_____

_____

_____

_____

_____

_____

How do you relate to the people of God? Where do you see yourself in relation to them—at the centre, on the edges, or somewhere else?

How would you like to see God bring renewal to your relations with other Christians?

What might be your part in seeing renewal come to the people of God in the place you live?

Renewal of the earth

Week Three

A glorious new creation

Sunday 16 December

Isaiah 65.17-25

¹⁷ For I am about to create new heavens
   and a new earth;
  the former things shall not be remembered
   or come to mind.
¹⁸ But be glad and rejoice for ever
   in what I am creating;
  for I am about to create Jerusalem as a joy,
   and its people as a delight.
¹⁹ I will rejoice in Jerusalem,
   and delight in my people;
  no more shall the sound of weeping be heard in it,
   or the cry of distress.
²⁰ No more shall there be in it
   an infant that lives but a few days,
   or an old person who does not live out a lifetime;
  for one who dies at a hundred years will be considered a youth,
   and one who falls short of a hundred will be considered accursed.
²¹ They shall build houses and inhabit them;
   they shall plant vineyards and eat their fruit.
²² They shall not build and another inhabit;
   they shall not plant and another eat;
  for like the days of a tree shall the days of my people be,
   and my chosen shall long enjoy the work of their hands.
²³ They shall not labour in vain,
   or bear children for calamity;
  for they shall be offspring blessed by the LORD—
   and their descendants as well.
²⁴ Before they call I will answer,
   while they are yet speaking I will hear.
²⁵ The wolf and the lamb shall feed together,
   the lion shall eat straw like the ox;
   but the serpent—its food shall be dust!
  They shall not hurt or destroy
   on all my holy mountain,
  says the LORD.

Prayer

Lord, may I be open to being your mouthpiece, your hands and your feet as you usher in your glorious new creation in words, works and wonders.

If you could change anything in this life, what would it be? Do these verses bring you hope for that change?

This passage builds on earlier verses (42.5-6; 48.6) that emphasise God as creator, who sustains his creation and promises new things.

Now we have the promise of glorious new heavens and a new earth, radically different from what has gone before. They are being renewed rather than replaced, and transformed rather than transplanted from elsewhere.

In this new order of God's rule, three key human relationships are renewed and transformed—relationships with God, with each other, and with the environment. There will even be harmony in the animal world. For God's people, there will be abundant joy, long life, the building of new homes, fruitful new vines, and fulfilling work. Premature death will be unknown. Such a long, full life would be perceived as a true blessing. And these blessings will be passed on to future generations. God will be intimately involved with and caring for his people.

These verses therefore complete God's own desire for Jerusalem (1.26 and 5.7), and the joy described of this wonderful promise is both God's and his people's. Do you see yourself as a joy and delight to the Lord?

There are allusions here to the beginning of creation; the tree in verse 22 echoes the tree of life in Genesis 2.9 and 3.22, one which is capable of giving eternal life. Similarly, here the snake is humiliated. With this sense of returning to origins in a vision of glorious hope, how might God be calling you to participate in his work of transformation, of restoring hope to a broken world?

James Webster

James worked in low-income countries on water, sanitation and hygiene projects, and as a consultant and University lecturer, before becoming an ordinand at St John's.

Past, present and future

Monday 17 December

Joel 2.18, 23-32

¹⁸ Then the LORD became jealous for his land,
and had pity on his people. [...]

²³ O children of Zion, be glad
and rejoice in the LORD your God;
for he has given the early rain for your vindication,
he has poured down for you abundant rain,
the early and the later rain, as before.
²⁴ The threshing-floors shall be full of grain,
the vats shall overflow with wine and oil.

²⁵ I will repay you for the years
that the swarming locust has eaten,
the hopper, the destroyer, and the cutter,
my great army, which I sent against you.

²⁶ You shall eat in plenty and be satisfied,
and praise the name of the LORD your God,
who has dealt wondrously with you.
And my people shall never again be put to shame.
²⁷ You shall know that I am in the midst of Israel,
and that I, the LORD, am your God and there is no other.
And my people shall never again be put to shame.

²⁸ Then afterwards I will pour out my spirit on all flesh;
your sons and your daughters shall prophesy,
your old men shall dream dreams,
and your young men shall see visions.
²⁹ Even on the male and female slaves,
in those days, I will pour out my spirit.

³⁰ I will show portents in the heavens and on the earth, blood and fire and columns of smoke. ³¹ The sun shall be turned to darkness, and the moon to blood, before the great and terrible day of the LORD comes. ³² Then everyone who calls on the name of the LORD shall be saved; for in Mount Zion and in Jerusalem there shall be those who escape, as the LORD has said, and among the survivors shall be those whom the LORD calls.

Prayer
Heavenly Father, in this Advent season help us to understand the hope that the baby in Bethlehem brings to us, and what this means for us today and for our future.

We were on our way to see some friends in Cambridge when I suddenly realised that my husband was talking about roads to Oxford. Yes, we were going in the wrong direction. We diverted and arrived at our friends a little late, much to their amusement!

Israel took several wrong turns on their journey with God; they did not think through their words and actions. These verses signify another turn for Israel. The previous verses talked of destruction, but here we move to words of restoration of the land and the people. We go from the dust of devastation to green shoots of hope and rejoicing. God again turns around circumstances and responds to the prayers of the people. God wants to give provision in abundance to his people. He wants to bring renewal to the whole of his creation and in return asks for the whole of his creation to praise him and rejoice.

Joel paints a breath-taking picture, pointing beyond the present to the future of what God will do. He will pour out his Spirit on all flesh; there will be no discrimination between men or women, old or young. The promise is for all.

That promise remains for you and for me today; God still wants to bring restoration and renewal to all people. Your past might have been full of devastation and destruction…perhaps your present is too. But God wants to restore and renew all aspects of creation, including each individual.

Today examine your heart and mind and ask Jesus where he might want to pour out his Spirit in your life. Then give him the freedom to do this and he will do more than we can ever imagine.

Sarah Hare
Sarah is married to Simon and is an ordinand from the Lichfield Diocese. She previously studied with Extension Studies at St John's before commencing ordination training in 2011.

Protection from the Lord of Hosts

Tuesday 18 December

Zechariah 8.1-13

[8] The word of the LORD of hosts came to me, saying: [2] Thus says the LORD of hosts: I am jealous for Zion with great jealousy, and I am jealous for her with great wrath. [3] Thus says the LORD: I will return to Zion, and will dwell in the midst of Jerusalem; Jerusalem shall be called the faithful city, and the mountain of the LORD of hosts shall be called the holy mountain. [4] Thus says the LORD of hosts: Old men and old women shall again sit in the streets of Jerusalem, each with staff in hand because of their great age. [5] And the streets of the city shall be full of boys and girls playing in its streets. [6] Thus says the LORD of hosts: Even though it seems impossible to the remnant of this people in these days, should it also seem impossible to me, says the LORD of hosts? [7] Thus says the LORD of hosts: I will save my people from the east country and from the west country; [8] and I will bring them to live in Jerusalem. They shall be my people and I will be their God, in faithfulness and in righteousness.

[9] Thus says the LORD of hosts: Let your hands be strong—you that have recently been hearing these words from the mouths of the prophets who were present when the foundation was laid for the rebuilding of the temple, the house of the LORD of hosts. [10] For before those days there were no wages for people or for animals, nor was there any safety from the foe for those who went out or came in, and I set them all against one another. [11] But now I will not deal with the remnant of this people as in the former days, says the LORD of hosts. [12] For there shall be a sowing of peace; the vine shall yield its fruit, the ground shall give its produce, and the skies shall give their dew; and I will cause the remnant of this people to possess all these things. [13] Just as you have been a cursing among the nations, O house of Judah and house of Israel, so I will save you and you shall be a blessing. Do not be afraid, but let your hands be strong.

Prayer

O Lord when we feel vulnerable and insecure help us to draw close to you and be assured of your closeness and loving care; when we feel like being aggressive because we feel under attack may we draw strength from our identity in you and overcome evil with good. Help us to play our part in rebuilding a sense of community and safety in the place where we live.

'Darling do you mind if I pop out to buy a newspaper while you sleep?" Yes' I sobbed. My dad was looking after me during a sick day off school when I was about eight years old. He wasn't physically caring for me in my bedroom, and I wasn't seriously ill but the thought of him leaving the house to go shopping made me feel vulnerable and weepy.

This passage from Zechariah was written after the time of exile when the people of Judah were beginning to return to their homeland to rebuild their lives and the temple. The LORD of hosts, a phrase used ten times in these verses, emphasises the fact that God is promising to stay close and be their protector. Through the prophetic words of Zechariah he is assuring them that from now on life is going to get better, once again Jerusalem will be a good place to grow up and grow old in. Old people will be able to sit in the streets in safety and parents will be happy to let their children play outside. What a picture of a content community living at ease with itself. What a picture of content individuals and families relaxing and enjoying intergenerational life together, when the Lord is in control and people are living according to his standards. That is what life can be like: 'You who live in the shelter of the Most High, who abide in the shadow of the Almighty, will say to the Lord, "My refuge and fortress; my God in whom I trust"' (Psalm 91.1–2).

Paula Preston

Paula was an ordinand at St John's from 2010 to 2012 and is currently serving her title as Assistant Curate in the parish of St. Martin, Cambridge.

Keep you head up—there is hope!

Wednesday 19 December

Romans 8.18-25

[18] I consider that the sufferings of this present time are not worth comparing with the glory about to be revealed to us. [19] For the creation waits with eager longing for the revealing of the children of God; [20] for the creation was subjected to futility, not of its own will but by the will of the one who subjected it, in hope [21] that the creation itself will be set free from its bondage to decay and will obtain the freedom of the glory of the children of God. [22] We know that the whole creation has been groaning in labour pains until now; [23] and not only the creation, but we ourselves, who have the first fruits of the Spirit, groan inwardly while we wait for adoption, the redemption of our bodies. [24] For in hope we were saved. Now hope that is seen is not hope. For who hopes for what is seen? [25] But if we hope for what we do not see, we wait for it with patience.

Prayer

Christ with me, Christ before me, Christ behind me;
Christ within me, Christ beneath me, Christ above me;
Christ to the right of me, Christ to the left of me
(From St Patrick's Breastplate)

As we go through today may we be focussed on Christ. He is the hope of future glory. Whatever circumstances we encounter today lift up your eyes and allow the Hope of Glory to sustain you and lead you.

We only have to open the papers to read stories of heartache, poverty, war, financial disaster and human failings. We live in a world, which as this passage says, is in bondage to decay groaning as it waits for change—hoping for a better future. The image of groaning in labour pains provokes interesting thoughts for me as a mother of five but what a brilliant picture of the joy that is to come after this present pain.

This passage calls us to stop and refocus our gaze. Whilst acknowledging the present suffering Paul says the situation is not hopeless. We are a people of hope. We have hope in a future that has been promised to us where there will be no pain and no more death (Revelation 21.4). If we lift our eyes and fix them on Jesus we will not lose heart but we will experience hope and the assurance of Christ in us and for us (2 Corinthians 4.18).

In the midst of suffering God gives us love and hope. Gifts we can give generously to others. In a world of suffering we have hope for now and hope for the future. In the same way that midwives encourage labouring mothers to keep their eyes fixed on what is to come, so too can we get alongside others and encourage them to stand firm in their suffering and to refocus their eyes on all that is to come.

What better gift can we give to others this Christmas as we wait patiently for all that is to come?

Sam Phillips

Sam is a second year Centre for Youth Ministry (CYM) student studying Schools, Youth and Community Work.

Citizens of heaven—and earth

Thursday 20 December

Philippians 3.17-4.1

[17] Brothers and sisters, join in imitating me, and observe those who live according to the example you have in us. [18] For many live as enemies of the cross of Christ; I have often told you of them, and now I tell you even with tears. [19] Their end is destruction; their god is the belly; and their glory is in their shame; their minds are set on earthly things. [20] But our citizenship is in heaven, and it is from there that we are expecting a Saviour, the Lord Jesus Christ. [21] He will transform the body of our humiliation so that it may be conformed to the body of his glory, by the power that also enables him to make all things subject to himself. [41] Therefore, my brothers and sisters, whom I love and long for, my joy and crown, stand firm in the Lord in this way, my beloved.

Prayer

Lord, as we look to your heavenly city, we pray for renewal in the cities of this world.

I have lived most of my Christian life in the inner city. There is much to renew there, but I have been struck by how many urban churches depict renewal in posters and slides of the countryside—of mountains, fields and cool, clear streams. Of course, these images appear in Scripture. Yet they can be misunderstood as suggesting that renewal is about retreating or escaping from the city and its concerns. At first sight here, Paul might seem to be suggesting something similar: our citizenship, he says, is in heaven. Yet that citizenship is meant to inform our engagement with the city now, not to deny it. Elsewhere, indeed, Paul is happy to affirm his earthly citizenship as an aid to mission (Acts 22.28). Just as Jeremiah urged Israel to 'seek the welfare of the city', Christian hope for renewal can never be hope for separation from those issues of governance, economics and justice that find their most concentrated expression in the urban context.

The New Jerusalem that will be our eternal home might be gloriously renewed, but it will still recognisably be Jerusalem. This continuity should make us more, not less concerned about present-day cities. Like Paul we might long to 'depart and be with Christ' (1.23), but as Paul also realised, until Jesus calls us home there is gospel work to do.

The Malt Cross project is a good example of this gospel work. It engages churches across Nottingham in ministry to the many thousands who flock to the city centre each weekend to participate in the night-time economy. Now, in a flourishing network of street pastors, non-alcoholic bars and temporary accommodation, Malt Cross brings the heavenly citizenship of its Christian staff and volunteers 'down to earth'. In doing so, it reminds all of us who follow Christ that our civic responsibilities apply here and now, and cannot simply be deferred to the coming age.

David Hilborn

David ministered and taught in the URC and the Church of England in Nottingham and London before being appointed Principal of St John's in 2012.

All things reconciled to God

Friday 21 December

Colossian 1.15-20

[15] He is the image of the invisible God, the firstborn of all creation; [16] for in him all things in heaven and on earth were created, things visible and invisible, whether thrones or dominions or rulers or powers—all things have been created through him and for him. [17] He himself is before all things, and in him all things hold together. [18] He is the head of the body, the church; he is the beginning, the firstborn from the dead, so that he might come to have first place in everything. [19] For in him all the fullness of God was pleased to dwell, [20] and through him God was pleased to reconcile to himself all things, whether on earth or in heaven, by making peace through the blood of his cross.

Prayer

Lord, all of our life experience is of this imperfect world. Please help us through your word to us today to catch just a glimpse of what a perfect life might be like. Inspire us by what we see and give us peace and hope for today.

Imagine the scene—a busy city centre. The camera pans slowly around our subject, who is moving in real time. All of the background is a blur of activity, filmed at high speed. The effect captures our imagination. The world around us is relentlessly busy and we struggle to find peace amongst the frenetic activity.

This world knows very little about genuine peace. Our planet faces the threat of global warming; our continent is being hit by financial and political crises; our nation is involved in wars; there is youth unemployment in our cities and, at an individual level, there is, unsurprisingly, widespread anxiety. Like others throughout history we live in the midst of these and so many other problems, many of which are of our own collective making.

This first century poem, written or quoted by Paul, is telling us about genuine peace—how and why it comes about and what it is like. Peace comes 'through the blood of the cross' (v. 20); through Jesus's offering of himself for us. It comes to reconcile us to God, but not just us—all things are reconciled to God. All of this created order has been at odds with God yet, in Jesus, God has done all that is needed for reconciliation. God has given his fullness (v. 19)—all that he has to give; it is as if we have had an argument and need to make up. But the very good news is that we now know that this reconciliation will happen. Definitely. It makes sense really—if all things are 'created through him and for him' (v. 16) then he is, of course, both willing and able to bring us and all of creation back into relationship with himself.

So to live with this peace we need to look to Jesus, 'the image of the invisible God' (v. 15), not just as a model of perfect humanity to emulate, but as our reconciler. He lived in this messy un-reconciled world, yet knew the peace that comes through obedience to his Father. And we need to entrust our futures to him. He is the 'firstborn from the dead' (v 18). In his resurrection, he is the promise, if you like, of the hope we have of resurrected life in a renewed, perfect world, reconciled to God.

Ponder

What makes you anxious about life as it is now?

What do you find the most exciting prospect about life in a perfect world?

Is there any area of your life that you need to bring into obedience in order to know God's peace?

Christopher Blunt

Chris has been a Civil Engineer and a Mission Partner working in community development in East Asia and is now an ordinand at St John's.

Review and reflect

_____

_____

_____

_____

_____

_____

_____

_____

_____

_____

_____

_____

_____

_____

_____

_____

_____

How important is the environment to you?

Do you see the wider world as part of God's creation?
Where do you long to see renewal happening?

In what ways is God challenging you to change your
lifestyle or priorities in order to reflect his love for
creation?

Personal
Week Four renewal

Renew a right spirit within me

Sunday 23 December

Psalm 51.1-12

[1] Have mercy on me, O God,
    according to your steadfast love;
  according to your abundant mercy
    blot out my transgressions.
[2] Wash me thoroughly from my iniquity,
    and cleanse me from my sin.

[3] For I know my transgressions,
    and my sin is ever before me.
[4] Against you, you alone, have I sinned,
    and done what is evil in your sight,
  so that you are justified in your sentence
    and blameless when you pass judgement.
[5] Indeed, I was born guilty,
    a sinner when my mother conceived me.

[6] You desire truth in the inward being;
    therefore teach me wisdom in my secret heart.
[7] Purge me with hyssop, and I shall be clean;
    wash me, and I shall be whiter than snow.
[8] Let me hear joy and gladness;
    let the bones that you have crushed rejoice.
[9] Hide your face from my sins,
    and blot out all my iniquities.

[10] Create in me a clean heart, O God,
    and put a new and right spirit within me.
[11] Do not cast me away from your presence,
    and do not take your holy spirit from me.
[12] Restore to me the joy of your salvation,
    and sustain in me a willing spirit.

Prayer

If you are able, set aside some time between now and Christmas Day to pray this psalm as a penitential prayer.

As I write, reminders of the sinful nature of humanity seem to loom large whichever way you turn—the Leveson inquiry into press standards; massacres in Syria; the Euro economic crisis to name but a few. Psalm 51, a penitential prayer, is a reminder to each of us of our need to repent of our sins if we are to make a new start with God (v.10).

The psalm begins with a cry for mercy from the penitent with three word pictures being used to describe his separation from God: He asks God to 'blot out' or erase from the record his offences; to thoroughly 'wash' him, that is to tread out his sins as in the oriental method of doing the laundry, and to 'cleanse' his sin, in the same way that impurities would be removed from metals.

The middle section of the psalm (vv. 6–14) forms the prayer for cleansing and spiritual renewal. The penitent cries out, 'purge me with hyssop' (v. 7), as though he were a leper needing the sprinkling of holy water. The prayer for forgiveness is repeated again and again, 'create in me a clean heart, put a new and right spirit within me.' The penitent recognises that a radical change needs to be wrought by God if the future is not to be a repetition of the past.

Verse 15 is well known to many as the opening lines of the Anglican liturgy for Morning Prayer. It is a hymn of praise which seems to follow a period of silence. It could be that the psalmist was unable to speak because of his broken relationship with God. This praise of God demonstrates deliverance and restoration. Verses 16 and 17 remind us that God requires no material gift from us, rather simply contrition and gratitude.

Kate Ellis

Kate is Personal Assistant to the Principal of St John's.

Heaven invades earth!

Monday 24 December

Mark 5.1-20

⁵ They came to the other side of the lake, to the country of the Gerasenes. ² And when he had stepped out of the boat, immediately a man out of the tombs with an unclean spirit met him. ³ He lived among the tombs; and no one could restrain him anymore, even with a chain; ⁴ for he had often been restrained with shackles and chains, but the chains he wrenched apart, and the shackles he broke in pieces; and no one had the strength to subdue him. ⁵ Night and day among the tombs and on the mountains he was always howling and bruising himself with stones. ⁶ When he saw Jesus from a distance, he ran and bowed down before him; ⁷ and he shouted at the top of his voice, 'What have you to do with me, Jesus, Son of the Most High God? I adjure you by God, do not torment me.' ⁸ For he had said to him, 'Come out of the man, you unclean spirit!' ⁹ Then Jesus asked him, 'What is your name?' He replied, 'My name is Legion; for we are many.' ¹⁰ He begged him earnestly not to send them out of the country. ¹¹ Now there on the hillside a great herd of swine was feeding; ¹² and the unclean spirits begged him, 'Send us into the swine; let us enter them.' ¹³ So he gave them permission. And the unclean spirits came out and entered the swine; and the herd, numbering about two thousand, rushed down the steep bank into the lake, and were drowned in the lake.

¹⁴ The swineherds ran off and told it in the city and in the country. Then people came to see what it was that had happened. ¹⁵ They came to Jesus and saw the demoniac sitting there, clothed and in his right mind, the very man who had had the legion; and they were afraid. ¹⁶ Those who had seen what had happened to the demoniac and to the swine reported it. ¹⁷ Then they began to beg Jesus to leave their neighbourhood. ¹⁸ As he was getting into the boat, the man who had been possessed by demons begged him that he might be with him. ¹⁹ But Jesus refused, and said to him, 'Go home to your friends, and tell them how much the Lord has done for you, and what mercy he has shown you.' ²⁰ And he went away and began to proclaim in the Decapolis how much Jesus had done for him; and everyone was amazed.

Prayer

Heavenly Father, we acknowledge that we are all in need of your renewal. Thank you that none of us is beyond redemption. Show us how to use that grace for your glory, in Jesus's name.

Christmas Eve, and we are on the cusp of celebrating heaven's invasion of earth in the shape of a baby wrapped in swaddling—our God of the unexpected and surprising. When Jesus visited the region of the Gerasenes and healed the demoniac there, heaven touched earth again. When heaven invades earth, all things are made new; healing and restoration follow. The demoniac went from living in a cemetery, naked and socially 'dead', to being dressed and sensible. There are very few more dramatic personal transformations in the Bible. It shows us that there is always the possibility of total personal renewal, and that no one is beyond the rescue of our King.

Heaven-sent renewal is always for a purpose. It will leave us feeling better about ourselves, but that is not the final goal. Jesus healed the demoniac and would not let him follow him—he was to stay and tell the others his story. He became the first missionary to the Gentiles.

The reactions of the others—both in Luke's Christmas story and in this one—also have something to teach us. The shepherds are first afraid, then joyful, spreading the word about what they had seen. There is little indication that the people of the Gerasenes were particularly disturbed by the chain-breaking, self-harming demoniac living outside the town, but when they see heaven's healing power they are frightened and beg Jesus to leave.

The question is how do we react to divine surprises? Will we be afraid of heaven's power or others' reactions? Or will we embrace the transforming power of heaven on earth, and share our stories and the good news with others in joy—like the shepherds and the former demoniac?

Ponder

Think about what your story or stories of heavenly renewal are. Thank God for this heaven-invasion in your life and pray for opportunities to share what God has done.

Evelyn Sweerts

Evelyn is a part-time student studying Theology for Ministry by distance learning at St John's.

I love you. I trust you. Follow me.

Tuesday 25 December

John 21.15-19

[15] When they had finished breakfast, Jesus said to Simon Peter, 'Simon son of John, do you love me more than these?' He said to him, 'Yes, Lord; you know that I love you.' Jesus said to him, 'Feed my lambs.' [16] A second time he said to him, 'Simon son of John, do you love me?' He said to him, 'Yes, Lord; you know that I love you.' Jesus said to him, 'Tend my sheep.' [17] He said to him the third time, 'Simon son of John, do you love me?' Peter felt hurt because he said to him the third time, 'Do you love me?' And he said to him, 'Lord, you know everything; you know that I love you.' Jesus said to him, 'Feed my sheep. [18] Very truly, I tell you, when you were younger, you used to fasten your own belt and to go wherever you wished. But when you grow old, you will stretch out your hands, and someone else will fasten a belt around you and take you where you do not wish to go.' [19] (He said this to indicate the kind of death by which he would glorify God.) After this he said to him, 'Follow me.'

Prayer

Lord speak to me through your living Word, as I in my imperfect humanity say to you the only true God 'I love you and I will follow you'.

'Three times' my driving instructor said. 'Always flash your indicator three times; one flash and other drivers will barely notice, two flashes and they start to engage their brain cells. Only after three flashes do they realise what's going on'.

I guess it is human nature that often we need three reminders before things start to make sense, and so it appears for Peter. Of course Peter had mucked up, not once, or twice, but three times. He had denied Jesus to save his own skin, compounded by his assertion earlier that he would die for Jesus (John 13.37). I love the way we see Peter 'warts and all'. He is a flawed human like us and yet God commissions him to lead the church.

Like Peter, I know I have failed in many different situations; I have promised so much and then not delivered. But our God is not an 'I-told-you-so' God. He is a God of renewal and rebirth. He wants to tell us daily;

> 'Feed my lambs—I trust you.'
> 'Tend my sheep—I want to invest in you.'
> 'Feed my sheep—I know you will get things wrong, but when you stop
> relying on yourself, then you will totally rely on me.'

We need to hear these words for ourselves—that God loves us and has entrusted to us the continuation of Jesus's mission, begun in a stable, to bring in his kingdom wherever we are and whomever we are with. As we follow Jesus, we need to make God's love known. It might take three words. It might take three minutes. It might take three years walking alongside someone, but it will be worth it.

Ponder

Take some time to listen to God telling you, 'I love you', 'I trust you'. You might start by picking out three Bible verses that speak of God's love to you, and then read each one three times.

Stephen Partridge

Stephen is an Anglican ordinand studying at St John's College and making the exciting transition from infant school teacher into church leader whilst remaining a husband, father and son.

The cornerstone—renew us by your Spirit

Wednesday 26 December

Acts 4.5-16

[5] The next day their rulers, elders, and scribes assembled in Jerusalem, [6] with Annas the high priest, Caiaphas, John, and Alexander, and all who were of the high-priestly family. [7] When they had made the prisoners stand in their midst, they inquired, 'By what power or by what name did you do this?' [8] Then Peter, filled with the Holy Spirit, said to them, 'Rulers of the people and elders, [9] if we are questioned today because of a good deed done to someone who was sick and are asked how this man has been healed, [10] let it be known to all of you, and to all the people of Israel, that this man is standing before you in good health by the name of Jesus Christ of Nazareth, whom you crucified, whom God raised from the dead. [11] This Jesus is

"the stone that was rejected by you, the builders;
      it has become the cornerstone."

[12] There is salvation in no one else, for there is no other name under heaven given among mortals by which we must be saved.'

[13] Now when they saw the boldness of Peter and John and realized that they were uneducated and ordinary men, they were amazed and recognized them as companions of Jesus. [14] When they saw the man who had been cured standing beside them, they had nothing to say in opposition. [15] So they ordered them to leave the council while they discussed the matter with one another. [16] They said, 'What will we do with them? For it is obvious to all who live in Jerusalem that a notable sign has been done through them; we cannot deny it.

Prayer

Heavenly Father teach us to walk in your ways, to be renewed by your Spirit each and every day as we follow your Son Jesus.

I read this passage with my son Nathan who is twelve, and two things jumped out for us.

The first thing is that a cornerstone is important! In the structure of a building it is critical. It is crucial. It cannot be missed out, and without it the building cannot stand. It is the stone that takes the weight of the building. Without it the building would lose its integrity and our Christian lives are like this too. We are created to be in relationship with God, to have him at the centre of our lives, the cornerstone that we rely on and lean upon. There is no one that is more central to the building of our Christian life than Jesus.

My son made the second point. Peter and John were ordinary—nothing special in themselves, but they had been with Jesus, which made all the difference. They were not great speakers with deep scriptural and theological understanding from having been to college and studied forever. But they had spent three years learning from Jesus, and they were filled with the Holy Spirit. These unschooled men were given the words they needed at that time and in that place, having faithfully followed Jesus's teaching to heal the sick and to make disciples.

The disciples kept Jesus as their cornerstone and received boldness through walking with him through the Holy Spirit.

Ponder

Is Jesus the cornerstone of your life, or do you feel there is something missing?

As you step out in Jesus's name, what does the Holy Spirit want to do through and in you?

Katie Reeves

Katie is an Anglican ordinand studying at St John's with her husband. She has two boys; her youngest, Nathan, helped to write this reflection.

Diplomatic immunity

Thursday 27 December

2 Corinthians 5.16-21

[16] From now on, therefore, we regard no one from a human point of view; even though we once knew Christ from a human point of view, we know him no longer in that way. [17] So if anyone is in Christ, there is a new creation: everything old has passed away; see, everything has become new! [18] All this is from God, who reconciled us to himself through Christ, and has given us the ministry of reconciliation; [19] that is, in Christ God was reconciling the world to himself, not counting their trespasses against them, and entrusting the message of reconciliation to us. [20] So we are ambassadors for Christ, since God is making his appeal through us; we entreat you on behalf of Christ, be reconciled to God. [21] For our sake he made him to be sin who knew no sin, so that in him we might become the righteousness of God.

Prayer

Today Lord, make us worthy to be your ambassadors. Make us steadfast and strong in your power; and may we today represent you well in all our thoughts, words and actions

When, as a child, my class went on school trips we were always told to behave well and not do anything naughty, because while we out we were representing our school. The word 'ambassador' was thrown around to give a sense of grandeur to having to wear our school uniform when we were at the zoo.

As Christians we are ambassadors to Christ in everything we do. While we might not wear a uniform or any kind of label that connects us to the church, often others will attach labels to us. As a youth worker I am privileged both to live and work in the same community. As a Christian (and often the only one that many young people I encounter see) I have the responsibility to represent my faith in the same way that Jesus would represent it. This is not easy. The fortunate thing, Paul says, is that when we become followers of Christ, not only do we gain the burden (or privilege) to represent Christ, but we are renewed! 'The old life is gone. A new life has begun!' (New Living Translation). God gives us a new life, a new outlook on things and a new perspective on the world.

As Christians we are all called to represent Christ in all that we do, pointing away from ourselves to Jesus. As we live and work and play, we will be part of the process of reconciling people to God.

Ponder

Is there still something of the 'old you' that you try to cling onto? What can you do about that?

Thomas Spicer

Thomas is a second year student on the Midlands Centre for Youth Ministry (MCYM) Schools, Community and Youth Work degree. He lives and works in Quinton, Birmingham.

A tale of two bodies

Friday 28 December

Romans 12.1-8

¹ I appeal to you therefore, brothers and sisters, by the mercies of God, to present your bodies as a living sacrifice, holy and acceptable to God, which is your spiritual worship. ² Do not be conformed to this world, but be transformed by the renewing of your minds, so that you may discern what is the will of God—what is good and acceptable and perfect.

³ For by the grace given to me I say to everyone among you not to think of yourself more highly than you ought to think, but to think with sober judgement, each according to the measure of faith that God has assigned. ⁴ For as in one body we have many members, and not all the members have the same function, ⁵ so we, who are many, are one body in Christ, and individually we are members one of another. ⁶ We have gifts that differ according to the grace given to us: prophecy, in proportion to faith; ⁷ ministry, in ministering; the teacher, in teaching; ⁸ the exhorter, in exhortation; the giver, in generosity; the leader, in diligence; the compassionate, in cheerfulness.

Prayer

Lord, let your transforming power renew our whole being, as we meditate on your Word.

I wonder how you feel about your body? A lot of us have a negative body image, and are not particularly fond of looking in the mirror! But God loves your body—he made it, and he wants all of you, including your body, as a living sacrifice.

The idea of presenting the body to God would have surprised Greek readers, who often separated spiritual and physical, considering the spiritual to be better. But our bodies are holy and acceptable—when they are sacrificed to God and brought under his control, through the renewing of our minds. What happens in our hearts and minds is expressed in the actions of our bodies—for good or bad. We need to be changed from the inside out—transformed by the renewing of our minds so we 'may discern what is the will of God—what is good and acceptable and perfect'. As we are changed, the effects are shown by our physical body; in what we do and how we live our daily life.

Paul has spent the first eleven chapters explaining God's mercy, and now he says therefore—because of all this good news—your response should be...to present your whole self to God, and not, 'let the world around you squeeze you into its own mould' (v 2 J. B. Phillips).

But there is a second body mentioned in the passage: 'we, who are many, are one body in Christ'. Because we individually give our body and mind to God, we become part of the one Body—the Christian church, joined to all who are 'in Christ'. We belong to Christ and so we belong to one another. As the renewal of our mind affects the actions of our body, so it affects our relationships within the Body. Much of the outworking of our faith will be put into practice within the Body as we assess our gifts realistically and 'do what we can, not what we can't'. God has put within his body all the gifts needed—no one person needs to do it all, but we each need to do our bit. So let's offer our bodies and minds to be transformed for the good of the Body of Christ, and bring glory to his name.

Ponder

Is it the inside or outside of you that needs to be most sacrificed to God at the moment?

Is your contribution to the Body of Christ based on 'sober judgement' of yourself?

Maureen Collins

Maureen is full-time ordinand from Nottingham, with a wonderful family and diocese.

Review and reflect

_____

_____

_____

_____

_____

_____

_____

_____

_____

_____

_____

_____

_____

_____

In what areas of your life do you need to experience God's cleansing and renewing?

Where do you need to hear again God's good news of his love and presence?

Is there anything you need to leave behind as you recommit yourself to following him?

The renewal of hope

Week Five

Dancing skeletons

Sunday 30 December

Ezekiel 37.1-14

[37] The hand of the Lord came upon me, and he brought me out by the spirit of the Lord and set me down in the middle of a valley; it was full of bones. [2] He led me all round them; there were very many lying in the valley, and they were very dry. [3] He said to me, 'Mortal, can these bones live?' I answered, 'O Lord God, you know.' [4] Then he said to me, 'Prophesy to these bones, and say to them: O dry bones, hear the word of the Lord. [5] Thus says the Lord God to these bones: I will cause breath to enter you, and you shall live. [6] I will lay sinews on you, and will cause flesh to come upon you, and cover you with skin, and put breath in you, and you shall live; and you shall know that I am the Lord.'

[7] So I prophesied as I had been commanded; and as I prophesied, suddenly there was a noise, a rattling, and the bones came together, bone to its bone. [8] I looked, and there were sinews on them, and flesh had come upon them, and skin had covered them; but there was no breath in them. [9] Then he said to me, 'Prophesy to the breath, prophesy, mortal, and say to the breath: Thus says the Lord God: Come from the four winds, O breath, and breathe upon these slain, that they may live.' [10] I prophesied as he commanded me, and the breath came into them, and they lived, and stood on their feet, a vast multitude.

[11] Then he said to me, 'Mortal, these bones are the whole house of Israel. They say, "Our bones are dried up, and our hope is lost; we are cut off completely." [12] Therefore prophesy, and say to them, Thus says the Lord God: I am going to open your graves, and bring you up from your graves, O my people; and I will bring you back to the land of Israel. [13] And you shall know that I am the Lord, when I open your graves, and bring you up from your graves, O my people. [14] I will put my spirit within you, and you shall live, and I will place you on your own soil; then you shall know that I, the Lord, have spoken and will act, says the Lord.'

Prayer
Glory be to God whose power, working in us, can do infinitely more than we can ask or imagine (Ephesians 3.21).

One of the vivid memories I (Sally) have from my adolescence is a piece of contemporary dance I was involved in at school based on Saint-Saëns' Danse Macabre. I played a skeleton who comes to life at Halloween but goes back to the grave when the rooster crows at dawn—a few hours once a year is not much of a new life! Later, I came across this passage in Ezekiel and became captivated by a vision of hope offering new life to dry bones.

Commentators suggest that there are at least three ways we can look for hope in this passage. The first is the hope of resurrection after death. The second is hope for the dry bones of the church to become living bones. The third is hope for the renewal of individuals as the Holy Spirit, the breath of God, enters in and brings life to places where there has been death.

Approaching a new year is a good time to reflect on the dry bones to which we want to prophesy. Our New Year resolutions are often crafted in the hope that they may bring life to the dry bones in our lives but often that hope is faded in weeks, if not days. Perhaps this is because we put hope in our own abilities and our capacity for self-control, rather than drawing on hope that is rooted in God.

As Martin Luther King Jr. said, 'we must accept finite disappointment, but never lose infinite hope'. As we reflect on Ezekiel's vision we need to hold on to infinite hope; we need to listen to the voice of God, as he calls us to prophesy to the dry bones in our lives, our churches and our communities, in the expectation that we may see disappointment turn to joy.

Ponder
For which areas or issues do you need God to give you hope that you may see life in the dry bones? Take time to pray for them now.

Revd Dr Sally Nash and **Revd Paul Nash**
Sally is Director of the Midlands Centre for Youth Ministry based at St John's. Paul is a Tutor at Midlands Centre for Youth Ministry and Senior Chaplain at Birmingham Children's Hospital.

Fields shall again be bought in this land

Monday 31 December

Jeremiah 32.9-15

⁹ And I bought the field at Anathoth from my cousin Hanamel, and weighed out the money to him, seventeen shekels of silver. ¹⁰ I signed the deed, sealed it, got witnesses, and weighed the money on scales. ¹¹ Then I took the sealed deed of purchase, containing the terms and conditions, and the open copy; ¹² and I gave the deed of purchase to Baruch son of Neriah son of Mahseiah, in the presence of my cousin Hanamel, in the presence of the witnesses who signed the deed of purchase, and in the presence of all the Judeans who were sitting in the court of the guard. ¹³ In their presence I charged Baruch, saying, ¹⁴ Thus says the LORD of hosts, the God of Israel: Take these deeds, both this sealed deed of purchase and this open deed, and put them in an earthenware jar, in order that they may last for a long time. ¹⁵ For thus says the LORD of hosts, the God of Israel: Houses and fields and vineyards shall again be bought in this land.

Prayer

Father in Heaven, thank you that your investment in us, which cost you everything, can yield heavenly returns. Help us to be bold enough to invest our lives in others for the sake of your kingdom come.

How will we remember 2012? We will, of course, remember a number of things, such as the Queen's Jubilee, the Olympics and the top stories that dominated the news. There seemed an endless succession of depressing stories—the economy, the News International trial, as well as a number of European countries going out of business with the euro in crisis. Most of us have little interest in world markets and international politics but indirectly we have all been affected. Such big scale issues often leave us wondering who will actually sort it out—who can we trust and how will it all end?

For the people in exile during the time Jeremiah was writing, similar questions were being asked. For how long will the exile go on? Who will tell us what to do? Whom can we trust? Our passage falls in the centre of the book of Jeremiah sometimes known as the Book of Consolation. This is where Jeremiah unfolds the great promises of salvation the exiles have been longing to hear. He has told them of God's plans to settle them in the Promised Land. But first they need to make Babylon their home, pray for their enemies and wait…for seventy years.

Jeremiah was writing from prison. The Babylonian army was invading Jerusalem. Yet in the midst of his circumstances he has a vision from God; a clear instruction to buy a field from his cousin, in a place about to be occupied! Any financial advisor would be dissuading him, as the value of his investment would be unlikely to increase in the foreseeable future.

However to put our 'money where our mouth is' was as powerful an action then as it is today. We do not know how any crisis we are experiencing will end, but Jeremiah demonstrated his confidence in an all-knowing God. As a Prophet, he shared words inspired directly from God to meet some special need of the people, whether to warn, guide or console. Jeremiah spoke as one who knew God, his Law and Spirit.

Ponder

As we remember 2012 and prepare for a new year to come, let us place our trust in Jeremiah's God, who is the same yesterday, today and forever.

In what will you invest during the coming year?

Mo Trudel

Mo was commissioned from St John's this year and has begun her ministry as the Bishop of Stafford's Lay Chaplain to the Business Community. She has a desire to support Christians to fulfil their calling where God has placed them in the workplace.

New year, new day?

Tuesday 1 January

Luke 1.68-79

[68] 'Blessed be the Lord God of Israel,
    for he has looked favourably on his people and redeemed them.
[69] He has raised up a mighty saviour for us
    in the house of his servant David,
[70] as he spoke through the mouth of his holy prophets from of old,
[71] that we would be saved from our enemies and from the hand of all who hate us.
[72] Thus he has shown the mercy promised to our ancestors,
    and has remembered his holy covenant,
[73] the oath that he swore to our ancestor Abraham,
    to grant us [74] that we, being rescued from the hands of our enemies,
    might serve him without fear, [75] in holiness and righteousness
    before him all our days.
[76] And you, child, will be called the prophet of the Most High;
    for you will go before the Lord to prepare his ways,
[77] to give knowledge of salvation to his people
    by the forgiveness of their sins.
[78] By the tender mercy of our God,
    the dawn from on high will break upon us,
[79] to give light to those who sit in darkness and in the shadow of death,
    to guide our feet into the way of peace.'

Prayer

Father God, I pray that, however we feel today, by your Spirit we will experience afresh the hope you offer in your Son, Jesus Christ.

As you flick open the pages of this book, I wonder what emotions you are experiencing today? Worthy tiredness after a late night of parties? Enthusiastic anticipation with the dawning of a new year? Or inexplicable apathy after a painful year?

Zechariah's prophecy invites us to perceive again the new thing that has Jesus has done. He is the profound visitor who embodies and offers the salvation promised to the forefathers of the Old Testament. Luke urges us to dig deep into the wells of God's family to taste for ourselves the hope they clung onto—salvation from their enemies and the accomplishment of God's promise to Abraham. Luke also clearly shows us what membership in Jesus's family requires: exclusive, whole-life obedience. Nothing more. Nothing less.

So as a member of that family, how is your hope shaping up? Where, today, are you broken? Have your enemies overtaken you? Do you feel abandoned by God?

In my life there have been many times when my hope has been seemingly extinguished. The death of people close, the receiving of bad news, an anxious sense that God is absent and the fruit of the Kingdom is scarce. But somehow, by the Spirit of God, like a warming sunrise enveloping my skin, the eternal hope Jesus bought for us wells up within me. Whatever darkness you find yourself in, the daybreak is imminent. Throw yourself on Jesus; lose your life in him again.

Zechariah's prophecy would probably have been sung by the early church, and most certainly would have been sung with fervent and desperate hope. Like John (the child referred to in verse 76), who was the preliminary to Jesus and who proclaimed and waited patiently for this hope, we must persevere and find that song again, the hope found only in Jesus.

Ben Woodfield

Ben and his family were previously part of the Eden Network in Manchester. Ben is currently training as a pioneer minister at St John's.

Hope does not disappoint

Wednesday 2 January

Romans 5.1-5

⁵ Therefore, since we are justified by faith, we have peace with God through our Lord Jesus Christ, ² through whom we have obtained access to this grace in which we stand; and we boast in our hope of sharing the glory of God. ³ And not only that, but we also boast in our sufferings, knowing that suffering produces endurance, ⁴ and endurance produces character, and character produces hope, ⁵ and hope does not disappoint us, because God's love has been poured into our hearts through the Holy Spirit that has been given to us

Prayer

Glory be to God whose power, working in us, can do infinitely more than we can ask or imagine (Ephesians 3.21).

Today life returns to normal. The parties are all over. The drama of Christmas with its hype and indulgence have become memories, and now we face up to the reality of all that this new year offers. The excitement and anticipation of this season is often greater than the enjoyment. Is this what hope is all about? What have we left to look forward to?

Paul encourages us to look in the right direction when we hope for a new start or a fresh perspective. Knowing the facts of the matter—that we are made right with God by the generosity of the life and death of Jesus—we can know, without arrogance, the end of the matter too. Recognising the rough and the smooth of life, we can rejoice in the knowledge that God, the Master Weaver brings all our living together into a beautiful pattern, unimagined in the day to day of our living.

Paul writes that he boasts in the hope of the glory of God. If, as a later saint suggested, the glory of God is a human being fully alive, then we are encouraged into a great life, where our potential is realised, and our dreams come to fruition.

Ponder

Bring before God the areas of your life that disappoint you. As we accept and acknowledge these we are granted the courage to change our attitude to living.

What do you hope for? Is it in line with the love of God, as you know it now in your life at the moment?

Sarah Cawdell

Sarah is a tutor for Extension Studies at St John's. She lives with her family in Shropshire, and provides a place for reflection. Further writings can be found at www.fulcrum-anglican.org.uk

Called to one hope

Thursday 3 January

Ephesians 4.1-6

[4] I therefore, the prisoner in the Lord, beg you to lead a life worthy of the calling to which you have been called, [2] with all humility and gentleness, with patience, bearing with one another in love, [3] making every effort to maintain the unity of the Spirit in the bond of peace. [4] There is one body and one Spirit, just as you were called to the one hope of your calling, [5] one Lord, one faith, one baptism, [6] one God and Father of all, who is above all and through all and in all.

Prayer
May the God of hope fill us with all joy and peace in believing, so that we may abound in hope by the power of the Holy Spirit. (Romans 15.13)

When we say that we 'hope' for something, so often we are expressing a wishful, even wistful, desire. This is not the sense of hope that Paul has in verse four of today's reading. For Paul, in the crucifixion and resurrection of Jesus Christ, God has conquered death once and for all, and so offers us a sure and certain hope on which to build our lives. Our 'calling' (vv. 1, 4) refers here to the foundational calling of the gospel itself—summoning people to believe in Jesus as the risen Lord and king, and to give him their complete and undivided allegiance for the rest of their lives.

We are called to live out this hope, not as isolated individuals, but as a part of the one body (v. 4) that is the church. More particularly, the unity of the church is a key witness to the unity of the Christian hope. For this reason, Paul offers practical ways in which Christians ought to relate together (v. 2), and urges them to bind their lives together in peace (v. 3). In a world in which there are so many different Christian denominations, customs and practices, we must never lose sight of the call to hold tight to what we have in common (vv. 4-6), and to pray and work for the healing and reconciliation of Christ's body where it has become fractured.

Yet Christian hope, for Paul, is never a guarantee of comfort and tranquillity in this life; it is often quite the opposite. After all, Paul himself is writing these words from prison! Yet, interestingly, he notes his location as 'in the Lord' (v. 1), reflecting his sense of where the whole sphere of Christian living takes place, with his imprisonment to be seen as no exception. Similarly, in all the trials and tribulations that we may endure, there remains the promise that nothing 'will be able to separate us from the love of God in Christ Jesus our Lord' (Romans 8.39).

Ponder
To what extent does the call of Christ truly take precedence over all else in our lives? Are we passionate in prayer and action for unity of the church?

How far do we situate ourselves 'in the Lord', as opposed to in the ups and downs of daily life?

Mark Bradford
Mark is a third year ordinand at St John's and formerly a teacher. He supports Liverpool F.C. and is hoping for a better season than the last one!

Wedding wobblies

Friday 4 January

Revelation 21.1-7

²¹ Then I saw a new heaven and a new earth; for the first heaven and the first earth had passed away, and the sea was no more. ² And I saw the holy city, the new Jerusalem, coming down out of heaven from God, prepared as a bride adorned for her husband. ³ And I heard a loud voice from the throne saying,

> 'See, the home of God is among mortals.
> He will dwell with them;
> they will be his peoples,
> and God himself will be with them;
> ⁴ he will wipe every tear from their eyes.
> Death will be no more;
> mourning and crying and pain will be no more,
> for the first things have passed away.'

⁵ And the one who was seated on the throne said, 'See, I am making all things new.' Also he said, 'Write this, for these words are trustworthy and true.' ⁶ Then he said to me, 'It is done! I am the Alpha and the Omega, the beginning and the end. To the thirsty I will give water as a gift from the spring of the water of life. ⁷ Those who conquer will inherit these things, and I will be their God and they will be my children.

Prayer

Lord God, help us to remember your promise of mercy and love, looking forward to the day when we will dwell with you. Set your hope in our hearts so we can face the coming day.

I wonder if you have seen the programme 'Don't tell the Bride'. In this show the groom must choose every detail of the wedding for his bride-to-be. This includes the venue, cake, flowers and even the dress. He makes all the decisions with the bride only discovering the details on the day, sometimes with tears and sometimes with joy. It is a test of how well he knows her.

In this passage we read about the amazing plans that God has for his bride, the church. It is full of expressive language, showing the intimate relationship God wants with his people. As the groom, he has made all the arrangements. Unlike the TV programme, none of his plans will fail to impress or live up to grand expectations. There is a complete transformation of both earth and heaven for this new chapter in the relationship. He is making all things new—both the physical and the spiritual reality. The tools of suffering are dissolved in his kingdom, so the results of pain and death are removed forever. This is a place where we no longer struggle to find God in our lives, for he will be with us. It is an eternal promise of wondrous magnitude.

As we reach the end of this these readings and reflections, I wonder what you will take on from here. Maybe it will be the encouragement to continue to read the Bible daily, finding fresh words of wisdom for each coming day. Maybe you have been touched by a sense of renewal in your life. Whatever you have learnt and however you move on be assured that God's plans await us. We need to be patient and continue to deepen the special relationship with our perfect groom, the supreme ruler. The wedding preparations are underway.

Katie Cross

Katie is an ordinand at St John's and is married with three children.

Review and reflect

_____

_____

_____

_____

_____

_____

_____

_____

_____

_____

_____

_____

_____

_____

_____

_____

What do you hope for in the year to come? How can you place these hopes in the context of God's hope for the world?

Who do you know who needs to hear words of hope from you?

Are there ways in which you can be an agent of hope in your home, your neighbourhood, your workplace?

91

About St John's Nottingham

St John's College offers full-time, part-time and pioneer courses for ordinands, independent students and clergy, at Certificate, Foundation Degree, Honours, Masters and research levels. Creative and innovative training for mission-minded leaders integrates practical theology with biblical and theological learning to enable people to grow in their understanding and practice of discipleship in an evangelical and charismatic Anglican setting.

St John's Extension Studies provides full time and part time distance learning programmes of study in Theology and Ministry. We offer university validated programmes of study through the University of Chester and our own self-accredited courses.

Midlands Centre for Youth Ministry offers undergraduate and masters degrees in Youth and Community Work and Practical Theology which include nationally recognised professional accreditation and an optional schools specialism at undergraduate level, a BA in Children and Family Work and Practical Theology and accredited training in youth work for volunteers and a Foundation Degree in Community Based Pioneer Ministry.

Away Days, Conferences & Retreats
Away days, meetings, church groups and youth groups catered for. Full or part board. Chapel, library, dining room, quiet room, nursery, lounges, sports field on site. C of E; all welcome. Set within beautiful grounds in the historic village of Bramcote with nature reserve nearby.

Creative Christian Learning   *St John's contact details*

Enquiries
enquiries@stjohns-nottm.ac.uk   0115 9251114

Admissions
admissions@stjohns-nottm.ac.uk 0115 9683203

Development Director
h.taylor@stjohns-nottm.ac.uk   0115 9683221

Bookshop
bookshop@stjohns-nottm.ac.uk   0115 9683221

**St John's College
Chilwell Lane
Bramcote
Nottingham
NG9 3DS**

www.stjohns-nottm.ac.uk

Books and resources available from St John's

Faith for Life Series

The Distance Learner - A travel guide for Christians studying theology
Fit for the Purpose - The meaning of Christian vocation
In Search of Wholeness - A Christian theology of healing & practical training
The Vital Connection - A fresh approach to Christian spirituality
Cross Cultural Christian - How to live for God in another culture
Something in Common - An introduction to the practices of worldwide Anglicanism
God Thoughts - Engaging with the modern world,
Leading Children - A course for leaders of children's work
Sustaining the Earth - A Christian approach to caring for the environment
Look Both Ways - our Journey tThrough Life material repackaged

Publications

Women and Authority, Ian Paul
Explores the idea of hierarchy within gender relations

One Body in Christ, David Hilborn, Ian Randall
The History and Significance of the Evangelical Alliance

God and the Generations, David Hilborn, Matt Bird – Youth, Age and the Church Today

Movement for Change, David Hilborn – Evangelical Perspectives on Social Transformation

Fear and Trust, David Runcorn - Explores God-centred Leadership

Choice, Desire and the Will of God, David Runcorn - What More Do You Want?

Spirituality Workbook, David Runcorn - A guide for explorers, pilgrims and seekers

Angels, Andrew Angel
Ancient Whispers of Another World, - A thought-provoking introduction to angels

God Present but Unseen: The Message of Esther, David Firth

Presence, Power and Promise, David Firth - The Role of the Spirit of God in the Old Testament

Interpreting Deuteronomy: Issues and Approaches, David Firth, Philip Johnston

God, Sex, the Universe and All That, Roy McCloughry
Questions young people are asking about God

Youth Ministry: A Multi-faceted Approach, Sally Nash
Including chapters by Jo Whitehead and Paul Nash

Skills for Collaborative Ministry, Sally Nash, Jo Whitehead, Paul Nash
With useful tips & insights

Tools for Reflective Ministry, Sally Nash, Paul Nash – Reflecting theologically and spiritually

Introduction to Managing Yourself, Jo Whitehead
Time management, boundaries, stress, accountability

Supporting Dying Children and Their Families, Paul Nash – A Handbook for Christian Ministry

Everybody Welcome, Bob Jackson, George Fisher
The course where everybody helps grow their church

Common Worship Today-Study Edition, Mark Earey - A guide to Common Worship

Multi-Media Timeline

Christian Origins and **Modern Western Thought**, Tim Hull
Explore the cultural, intellectual and historical context of New Testament Christian Origins
and 20th Century theology. **http://stjt.org.uk/**

Programmes of study at St John's

Study with us full time for 1, 2 or 3 years or on a part-time basis.

*training for ordained/lay ministry - counselling courses - distance learning -
youth worker children & families worker training -
residential - occasional courses - away days*

Jan 7-28	*Four Week Module (Mondays).* Revelation as Counter-cultural Protest*. The *Revd Dr Ian Paul*
Feb 4-8	*In Service Study Week.* Understanding Church*. The *Revd Dr David Hilborn and members of Faculty*
Feb 11,25 and **Mar 4, 11**	*Four Week Module (Mondays).* Preaching Joshua as Christian Scripture*. The *Revd Dr David Firth*
Feb 20,27 and **Mar 6,13**	Going for Growth: *Wednesday afternoons 5-week course.* *The Venerable Bob Jackson*
Mar 18-22	*In Service Study Week.* The Bible in the Digital Age*. *The Revd Dr Pete Phillips*
Apr 8-12	Listening Skills. *A short skills-based course for those who want to become better listeners*
Apr 12-13	150th Anniversary Conference Charismatic Renewal & Mission
Apr 12-14	Fit for the Purpose Weekend. For anyone who feels that God is calling him or her...to what?
Apr 12-14	Myers Briggs Weekend. An introduction to personality type with reference to leadership and teamwork in the Christian context
Apr 15-19	*In Service Study Week.* Christian Apologetics in a Postmodern World*. *The Revd Dr Tim Hull*
Jul 1-5	*Summer school.* Top Up Your Theology Week. *Faculty share the latest developments in their subject areas.*
Jul 8-12	*Summer school.* Greek in a Week. *For those with a little Greek and a thirst for the Bible.*
Sep (tbc)	Centre for Church Growth Conference. *The Venerable Bob Jackson*

*For those with diploma level theology or equivalent

Programmes of study at St John's (continued)

Sep (tbc)	Heritage Open Days. *2-5pm Talks and tours of St John's historic building, The Grove.*
Sep 6-8	Counselling Skills for Pastoral Care. *Combining counselling skills, theology and personal growth (6-month course)*
Sep 14	Alumni reunion *to celebrate St John's 150th anniversary*
Sep 13-15 (tbc)	Fit for the Purpose Weekend. *For anyone who feels ~ that God is calling him or her...to what?*
Sep 20-22 (tbc)	Study Skills Weekend. *For those returning to academic study.*

Midlands Centre for Youth Ministry: Continuing Professional Development Courses

Jan 14-17	Chaplaincy. *The Revd Paul Nash*
Jan 14-15 and **Feb 11-12**	Play and Creativity. *Mrs Dawn O'Connell*
Mar 13-16	Religious Education. *Mr Nigel Roberts*
Mar 13-16	Training Skills. *The Revd Dr Sally Nash, Mrs Jo Whitehead, The Revd Paul Nash*

For details of all of these courses and an update on other events, please contact St John's (page 92)

A suite of events will be held throughout the year to celebrate St John's 150th anniversary. Please see our website for dates.

Practical support for St John's

The Church of England does not pay the full costs of the work of St John's, which has no historical endowment. We live by faith for the projects which make the learning at St John's distinctive, and are always praying for more funds to make these possible. We are grateful to God for the way in which he supplies our needs. If you would like to make a gift we would be glad to discuss this with you. Our commitments vary from continuing to improve computer and information technology, helping with special projects to enhance student learning and major building work to improve our facilities.

The Revd Dr David Hilborn, Principal

Ways to give

Donations
Make a regular gift or a one-off donation. Gift Aid your donations to St John's if you are a UK tax payer as we can claim an extra percentage for every £1 you give at no extra cost to you.

Leave a Legacy
Make a difference to future generations by including St John's in your Will—you will be playing your part in ensuring that the work of God stands forever and that the training of people for mission and ministry continues.

Give Online
Use our secure online form on our website to make a credit card gift to St John's— www.stjohns-nottm.ac.uk

Give Properties or Shares
Since St John's is a charity, transfers of capital assets for the benefit of the Development Fund do not incur liability to Capital Gains or Inheritance Taxes. Ask your broker to make an 'electronic transfer' of mutual fund or individual stock shares you wish to give.

Association Membership
Membership of the St John's College Association gives you a voice in the governance of St John's and allows you to contribute to the shape of the theological training in the future. There are many other benefits!

Through your Church
Invite us to preach or talk about training, pray for us, become a member and join our mailing list, plan fundraising events, recommend St John's, introduce us to Trusts, book your away days with us, contribute a regular amount from mission giving.

St John's is a registered charity no. 1026706